IT'S
NOT
ABOUT ME
ME
Journal

IT'S NOT ABOUT ME

Journal

MAX LUCADO

INTEGRITY®
PUBLISHERS
Nashville

Introduction

This companion journal to Max Lucado's *It's Not About Me* has been designed to help you grab hold of a God-centered life—and along with it, all the deep satisfaction and rich fulfillment that such a life alone offers. You can use the questions, Bible verses, and quotes in these fourteen entries not only to help you focus on the life-changing perspectives of *It's Not About Me*, but also to help you mull over how those perspectives might take root and blossom in your own life.

A few tips that have helped others to maximize their own journaling experience might help you as well:

As you prepare to write, get alone in a quiet, favorite spot. Some people like to play soft background music as they gather their thoughts.

Note the date of your journaling experience.

Some like to read a whole chapter before they begin writing. Others prefer to journal as they read, musing on the fresh ideas they encounter.

Be on the lookout for phrases, quotes, and Bible verses that especially grab your attention. Write them down and note your reaction to them.

Explore your feelings as well as your thoughts. Make this an adventure of self-discovery.

Don't be afraid to make lists or sketch out simple drawings.

Begin and end your journaling time with prayer, asking God to lead you into a life that truly satisfies.

When we make the awesome discovery that a God-centered life opens the door to astonishing possibilities, we begin to enjoy what we have longed for all our lives. "Life makes sense when we accept our place," writes Max. "The gift of pleasures, the purpose of problems—all for him. The God-centered life *works*. And it rescues us from a life that doesn't."

Happy journaling!

THE PUBLISHERS

But all of us who are Christians...reflect like mirrors the glory of the Lord.

2 CORINTHIANS 3:18 PHILLIPS

Q. What would a "God-centered" life look like for me?

"God raised him [Christ] from death and set him on a throne in deep heaven, in charge of running the universe, everything from galaxies to governments, no name and no power exempt from his rule. And not just for the time being but forever. He is in charge of it all, has the final word on everything. At the center of all this, Christ rules the church."

EPHESIANS 1:20–22 MSG

_____

_____

_____

_____

_____

_____

_____

_____

_____

_____

_____

_____

_____

_____

What Copernicus did for the earth,
God does for our souls. Tapping the
collective shoulder of humanity, God
points to the Son—his Son—and says,
"Behold, the center of it all."

MAX LUCADO

_____

_____

_____

_____

_____

_____

_____

_____

_____

_____

_____

*The God-centered life works. And it
rescues us from a life that doesn't.*

MAX LUCADO

Q.

HOW DO I BEST "SEE GOD'S FACE"? HOW DOES SEEING HIS FACE HELP ME TO HANDLE LIFE'S DIFFICULTIES?

"Show me your glory."

EXODUS 33:18 NCV

_____

_____

_____

_____

_____

_____

_____

_____

_____

_____

_____

*When our deepest desire is not the
things of God, or a favor from God,
but God himself, we cross a threshold.*

MAX LUCADO

You and I need what Moses needed—
a glimpse of God's glory.

M A X L U C A D O

Q.

IN WHAT WAYS
CAN I MOST EFFECTIVELY
REVEAL GOD'S GLORY?

*"Who among the gods is like you,
O LORD? Who is like you —
majestic in holiness, awesome in glory,
working wonders?"*

EXODUS 15:11 NIV

_____

_____

_____

_____

_____

_____

_____

_____

_____

_____

To seek God's glory is to pray,
"Let your nature spill forth.
God, show us God."

M A X   L U C A D O

Every act of heaven reveals
God's glory. Every act of Jesus
did the same.

MAX LUCADO

IF I WERE TO SEE GOD'S HOLINESS
AS GRAPHICALLY AS ISAIAH DID, WHAT IN
MY LIFE WOULD MOST LIKELY CHANGE? WHY?

"Holy, Holy, Holy, is the LORD of hosts,
The whole earth is full of His glory."

ISAIAH 6:3 NASB

_____

_____

_____

_____

_____

_____

God is not holy. He is not holy, holy.
He is holy, holy, holy.

M A X   L U C A D O

_____

_____

_____

_____

_____

_____

_____

_____

_____

_____

_____

_____

*Those who see God most clearly
regard him most highly.*

MAX LUCADO

Q. THINKING ABOUT ETERNITY—
AND THE GOD WHO DWELLS IN IT—
MIGHT HELP ME TO DEAL WITH MY
CURRENT PROBLEMS IN SEVERAL WAYS:

*"For thus says the High and Lofty One
who inhabits eternity, whose name is
Holy: 'I dwell in the high and holy
place, with him who has a contrite and
humble spirit, to revive the spirit
of the humble, and to revive
the heart of the contrite ones.'"*

ISAIAH 57:15 NKJV

_____

_____

_____

_____

_____

———————————————————————————

———————————————————————————

———————————————————————————

———————————————————————————

———————————————————————————

———————————————————————————

———————————————————————————

———————————————————————————

———————————————————————————

———————————————————————————

*Tucked away in each of us is a hunch
that we were made for forever,
and a hope that the hunch is true.*

MAX LUCADO

_The brevity of life grants
power to abide, not an excuse to bail._

M A X   L U C A D O

WHEN I CONSIDER HOW GOD

NEVER CHANGES,

IT MAKES ME FEEL . . .

*"The plans of the LORD
stand firm forever."*

PSALM 33:11 NIV

_____

_____

_____

_____

_____

_____

_____

_____

_____

_____

God will always be the same.
No one else will.

MAX LUCADO

His plan—born in eternity—
will withstand any attack of humanity.

MAX LUCADO

Q.

GOD REGULARLY SHOWS
HIS LIMITLESS LOVE TO ME BY . . .

*"I ask him [God] that with both feet
planted firmly on love, you'll be able to
take in with all Christians the
extravagant dimensions of Christ's love.
Reach out and experience the breadth!
Test its length! Plumb the depths!
Rise to the heights!"*

EPHESIANS 3:17–18 MSG

_____

_____

_____

_____

_____

_God's love . . . one swallow
slackens the thirsty throat and
softens the crusty heart._

M A X   L U C A D O

_____

_____

_____

_____

_____

_____

_____

_____

_____

_____

_____

_____

Does God love you? Behold the cross,
and behold your answer.

M A X   L U C A D O

Q. I FEEL MOST TEMPTED
TO GRAB THE GLORY THAT REALLY
BELONGS TO GOD WHEN . . .

*"And we, with our unveiled faces
reflecting like mirrors the brightness
of the Lord, all grow brighter and
brighter as we are turned into the image
that we reflect; this is the
work of the Lord who is Spirit."*

2 CORINTHIANS 3:18 JB

_____

_____

_____

_____

_____

Reduce the human job description
down to one phrase, and this is it:
Reflect God's glory.

M A X   L U C A D O

_____

_____

_____

_____

_____

_____

_____

_____

_____

_____

_____

_____

God sends the message; we mirror it.

MAX LUCADO

Q.

**WHAT MESSAGE ABOUT CHRIST
DO I COMMUNICATE TO OTHERS
BY THE WAY I LIVE?**

*"So the one who plants is not important,
and the one who waters is not
important. Only God, who makes
things grow, is important."*

1 CORINTHIANS 3:7 NCV

_____

_____

_____

_____

_____

_____

_____

_____

_____

_____

_____

_____

_____

_____

_____

_____

_____

_____

*I believe Satan trains battalions
of demons to whisper one question
in our ears: "What are
people thinking of you?"*

M A X   L U C A D O

_We who are entrusted with
the gospel dare not seek applause
but best deflect applause._

MAX LUCADO

IN WHAT WAY(S) DO I EVER TRY
TO "ADD" SOMETHING TO
THE SALVATION THAT CHRIST OFFERS ME?

*"God's way of making us right
with himself depends on faith—
counting on Christ alone."*

PHILIPPIANS 3:9 TLB

_____

_____

_____

_____

_____

_____

_____

Legalists trust in Christ a lot.
But they don't trust in Christ alone.

M A X   L U C A D O

Your salvation showcases
God's mercy. It makes nothing of your
effort but everything of his.

M A X   L U C A D O

HOW DO I USE MY BODY
TO GLORIFY GOD? WHEN DO I FEEL
MOST TEMPTED TO USE IT TO DISHONOR HIM?

*"You are no longer your own.
God paid a great price for you. So use
your body to honor God."*

1 CORINTHIANS 6:19–20 CEV

_____

_____

_____

_____

_____

_____

_____

Your body is God's instrument,
intended for his
work and for his glory.

M A X   L U C A D O

_____

_____

_____

_____

_____

_____

_____

_____

_____

_____

_____

_____

*If forced to choose, take the
soft heart over the hard body.*

MAX LUCADO

Q. I SEE NOW THAT GOD HAS USED
MY TROUBLES IN THE PAST YEAR
TO SHOW HIS GLORY IN THE FOLLOWING WAYS:

"Trust me in your times of trouble,
and I will rescue you,
and you will give me glory."

PSALM 50:15 NLT

_____

_____

_____

_____

_____

_____

_____

_____

_____

_____

_____

_____

_____

_____

_____

_____

_____

Is there any chance, any possibility,
that you have been
selected to struggle for God's glory?

MAX LUCADO

_____

_____

_____

_____

_____

_____

_____

_____

_____

_____

_____

_____

Your faith in the face of suffering
cranks up the volume of God's song.

MAX LUCADO

HOW HAVE I USED MY RECENT PERSONAL SUCCESSES TO SHOW OTHERS THE GREATNESS OF GOD?

"Always remember that it is the LORD your God who gives you power to become rich, and he does it to fulfill the covenant he made with your ancestors."

DEUTERONOMY 8:18 NLT

_____

_____

_____

_____

_____

_____

God lets you excel
so you can make him known.

M A X   L U C A D O

_Your success is not about
what you do. It's all about God—
his present and future glory._

Q. THIS WEEK, HOW CAN I
GIVE HONOR TO GOD'S NAME?

*"We are ambassadors for
Christ, as though God were making
an appeal through us."*

2   C O R I N T H I A N S   5 : 2 0   N A S B

_____

_____

_____

_____

_____

_____

_____

_____

_____

_____

_____

_____

_____

_____

_____

_____

_____

*Tucked away in the ceremonies
and laws of Moses are pictures of God.*

MAX LUCADO

_____

_____

_____

_____

_____

_____

_____

_____

_____

_____

_____

*May we have no higher goal
than to see someone think more highly
of our Father, our King.*

MAX LUCADO